CONTENTS

Words in **bold** appear in
the glossary on page 31.

THE SHAKING EARTH

When an earthquake strikes, the ground under your feet suddenly shakes, as rocks beneath the Earth's surface shift and tear.

Moving plates

The Earth is covered in a layer of rock called the crust. The crust forms the land and the floor of the oceans and is divided up into lots of pieces called **plates**.

The Earth's plates move very slowly – only one or two centimetres each year. Sometimes the edges of the plates jostle together. Pressure builds up as they push and grind against each other with great force. When this pressure is released, the land above shakes suddenly, causing an earthquake.

Earthquake zones

Earthquakes are more likely to happen in some parts of the world than others. Because most earthquakes happen where the Earth's plates meet, the countries that lie along these boundaries are more likely to suffer earthquakes (see map opposite). The cracks in the crust where the plates move against each other are called **faults**. Most of these faults are under the oceans and seas. But some of them can be seen on land, such as the **San Andreas Fault** in California in the United States.

▼ *A car in the port of Kobe stands with its back wheels in the air. An earthquake in this Japanese city in 1995 ripped up roads and flattened buildings.*